TREASURES IN HEAVEN

GOD, MONEY AND YOU

BOOK 4

ZACHARIAS TANEE FOMUM

books4revival.com

Unless stated otherwise, the version of the Bible used in this book is the Revised Standard Version.

Published by

books4revival.com

A division of the Book Ministry of Christian Missionary Fellowship International

info@books4revival.com

CONTENTS

PREFACE

Treasures in Heaven by Professor Zacharias Tanee Fomum, is a compelling work originally delivered as a message on February 7, 2006, in Obili, Yaounde. Within these pages, the author delves into two pivotal topics:

1. **Debts (loans):** Professor Fomum unveils God's perspective on debts and loans, drawing insights from both Scripture and personal experiences. He convincingly portrays loans as a tool of the devil, employed to ensnare God's children and hinder their qualification for the rapture, and ultimately, their entry into heaven. However, he doesn't leave readers in a state of despair; he provides a path to liberation from the shackles of debt.
2. **Giving to God (tithes and offerings):** The author passionately underscores the obligation of all believers to give tithes and offerings, supported by biblical references. He emphasizes the choice individuals face: to give and receive blessings or

> withhold and risk falling under a curse. The core message is that one's capacity to give is a reflection of the heart's disposition.

In the context of tithing, God issues a challenge: "Put me to the test." Professor Fomum's own testimony, shared in this book, serves as irrefutable evidence that those who give to God experience boundless blessings, validating God's promises.

This timely message is intended for all who have been "twice born," seeking spiritual renewal and growth. As we present this book, our prayer is that God will use it as a tool of liberation, freeing His children from the clutches of debt and the spectre of poverty. Moreover, we beseech Him to lead many towards experiencing His abundant blessings by opening the floodgates of heaven to those who obey and remain faithful.

May God's abundant blessings enrich your life as you engage with this profound work.

1

A DETERMINANT START IN THE WALK WITH GOD

Very early in the Christian life, a person decides what he will become. Whether he will take the upper pathway or the lower one, is determined then. John Wesley said that right from the day when someone comes to the Lord Jesus Christ, two pathways are open to him. We may represent them as below:

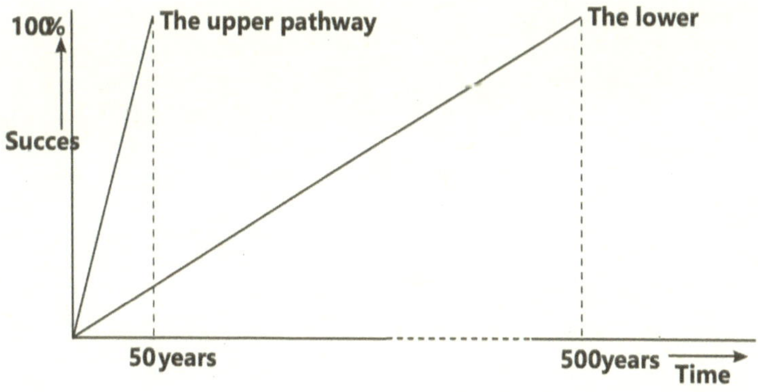

It means that the person who chooses the lower pathway needs 500 years to accomplish what the person who chooses the upper pathway will accomplish in 50 years. The pathway taken is a choice that is made from the beginning; but it is a choice that at each step is confronted anew. That choice may be made by one's attitude to a certain sin.

Research has shown that when a person comes to Christ, the sin he commits in the next twenty-four hours could cling to him all his life. He will battle with that sin all his life. The sin that a person commits during the first twenty-four hours with God seems to be engraved in his spiritual person, such that getting rid of it may be a life-long story. Freedom will require mighty acts because it will not be easy for the person to be set free.

In like-manner, the sin that a person commits after he has been baptised into the Holy Spirit entangles him almost permanently. What a person abandons on the day of his new birth tends to be abandoned forever. The first time a person deliberately goes to sin after he is born again, he has gone into a tragedy of tragedies.

2

THE BELIEVER AND LOANS

I read a book by an American. He says that for a believer who has taken a loan, if the church does not meet to deliver him, he may be a debtor till his death, moving from one debt to another. In fact, he says that only the church can deliver a man who goes into debts after he has believed. He says that even if you pay his debts for him, he will go into new ones. I was surprised that the book comes from America where people are encouraged to take loans.

Are you a debtor? Do you owe somebody? If you do, my beloved, you have cursed yourself. The elders of the church must arrange for a day of deliverance, if not, you will never come out of debts. You have cursed yourself. The curse will continue until a great force, the power of the church, comes to your deliverance.

Furthermore, your children will get into debts. Your grandchildren and great grandchildren will enter into debts. You have provided a spiritual code for your progeny. It will continue.

About ten years ago, a brother outside of the city of Yaounde needed four hundred thousand francs. My wife and I gave him the four hundred thousand francs so that he should not go into debts. He took the money, and still went into debts. The last time I met him, he was four million francs into debts.

3

DELIVERING THE DEBT-BOUND

I recommend that the church should arrange a deliverance ministry to deliver those who have cursed themselves with loans. If the church does it, there will be hope. If not, it will stretch to their wives and children. In one of the churches associated with our ministry, the man was paying debts which his wife took without his knowledge.

I want to beg you to say, "No" to that sin. You may not be able to come out of it. I want to beg you, do not enter into that sin, you may not be able to get out of it. When later on you find this same sin in your children, a knife will go into your heart with unceasing pain. There is nothing as painful as when your children whip you for your sins by committing the same sins. There is nothing as painful as when your children exaggerate your sin and trash you with it. When you see them commit it, you will say, "That is me. But I did not go this far." Each successive generation exaggerates the sins of the past generation.

I am told that our great grandfather was a lover of groundnuts. My grandfather was a lover of groundnuts and my father a lover of groundnuts. As a parliamentarian, my elder brother dried groundnuts at the balcony of his usual hotel room. My father never loved groundnuts that have been cracked already. He loved cracking them himself. For who he was, my elder brother could have bought already-cracked groundnuts. But he did not like those. He wanted those that he cracked himself. Three days ago one of our sons also went to look for "uncracked" groundnuts for me.

Listen, whatever you do, you are doing it for the coming generations. You have taught your children that one lives by being in debt. You have told them that God is not enough. Just wait and see. I have recommended that the local church should organise a deliverance meeting for those in debts. But you cannot deliver someone who does not want to be delivered. May God grant you to desire and seek deliverance.

I am persuaded with all my heart that anything for which a loan should be taken for it to be done is either not the will of God or it may not yet be God's time to do it.

4

DEBTS AND THE RAPTURE

My beloved, the trumpet could sound any time from now. How can a debtor be raptured? He must remain.

In the late seventies and early eighties, the whole matter of the return of the Lord was permanent on our hearts. Yesterday, a sister told me the following in relation to the rapture at the time, "We had been taught on the rapture, the fact that believers will all be taken to heaven when Jesus comes. What another sister and I understood was that all that one needed was to have received Jesus in his heart and he will be taken to heaven. Also, we had been taught that the rapture will come at a time when no one knew. So this sister and I said we would like to borrow money and things from people and enjoy ourselves, and when the trumpet sounds, we will be gone". It was a false assurance.

This kind of thinking amounts to transforming the God of heaven into a crook. People do not know God. They do not know what heaven is all about. To think that heaven will be a place where thieves go and hide, having run away from their creditors and from the things that they have snatched from people, is to miss it all.

In the US, an astronaut calculated and gave the date when Jesus was to return. There were brethren who said they will not pay their rents. Some thought of how not to pay the school fees of their children, thinking that on that day they will be gone. It is a matter of the corrupt heart, of the lost heart, separated from the grace of God and from the knowledge of God. It betrays a lack of the knowledge of who God is and what heaven is.

5

WHEN INIQUITY INCREASES

I am presently meditating on the book of the Acts of the Apostles. I finished meditating on John's gospel after six years. In Acts chapter one, I was just meditating on Jesus being taken up to heaven. As the disciples saw Him go, the angel said He will come back in the same manner. Then I began to ask the Lord, "Whom are you coming for?" I asked this question on the 2nd, but since then I am on this question till today the 7 of February 2006. It is producing utter fear in me.

At the same time, I am reading *The Pilgrim's Progress* by John Bunyan. I recommend it to you with all my heart. There is a false assurance for multitudes who will never enter the celestial City. It is such that there is freedom to sin, love the world, love the things of the world, and play about.

Let me read to you the verse that came as part of my meditation yesterday.

> *"Because of the increase of wickedness, the love of many will grow cold."* (Matthew 24:12)

Is this not where we are now? Iniquity has increased, hasn't it? Yesterday, my boss said three times over, "The world is finished. The world is finished. The world is finished." He was talking because of this increase in wickedness. This increase has caused the love of many to grow cold.

6

TITHING

The case of the Church in Yaounde

In the church in Yaounde, only 45% of the people gave a tithe last year, 2005[1]. This is evidence of love grown cold. What it means is that more than 55% of the church is under a curse. The person who withholds a tithe and an offering has cursed himself. When more than 55% of a local church, where the truth is taught, curse themselves by not regularly giving their tithes and offerings, there is increase in wickedness, because money is directional.

May the elders of the church in Yaounde see that more than 55% of the church is under a curse because of the fact that less than 45% faithfully give a tithe every month. May everyone know that by not giving their tithes and offerings, they have cursed themselves.

7

TITHING OR A CUSRE: CHOOSE

You may want to know from where we get the fact of being under a curse for failing to give one's tithes and offerings. Let us read from Malachi 3: 6-12:

> *"I the Lord do not change. So you, o descendants of Jacob, are not destroyed. Ever since the time of your forefathers you have turned away from my decrees and have not kept them. Return to me, and I will return to you;" says the Lord Almighty. "But you ask 'How are we to return?' "Will a man rob God? Yet you rob me. But you ask, 'How do we rob you?' In tithes and offerings. You are under a curse - the whole nation of you - because you are robbing me. Bring the whole tithe into the storehouse, that there may be food in my house. Test me in this," says the Lord Almighty, "and see if I will not throw open the floodgates of heaven and pour out so much blessing that you will not have room enough for it. I will prevent pests from devouring your crops, and the vines in your fields will not cast their fruit," says the Lord Almighty. "Then all the nations will call you blessed, for yours will be a delightful land," says the Lord Almighty.*

The believer must return to God in order that the task of evangelism, soul-winning and church-planting may be a life-giving process. The first way to return to God is to return to Him in giving. This is because money is directional. What has not happened to a man's money, has not happened to his heart. God says, "Return to me, and I will return to you." Then they ask, "How are we to return?" God did not say, "In your prayers." He did not say, "Return to me in fiery prayer." I am all in for fiery prayers, but that is not what God says.

God did not say, "Return to me in forty-day fasting." I am all in for forty-day fasting, but that was not the way back to God. No one should say, "I cannot pray fiery prayers and I cannot fast for forty days." You can do both and be a thief, stealing God's tithes. You may eat God's tithes and say, "Well, I have been fasting, so I can use the Lord's tithe to eat and rebuild my body. God understands." You may say, "God, I used my tithes to buy calcium so as to fast for You, O God." That makes you all the same into a thief, into a cursed person.

How are we to return? How are you to return? How is the church to return to God? How are individuals to return to God? When the people asked God this question, He answered. There is an answering God. Then God took them to task: Will a man rob God? And the answer is, "Yet you rob me." Then they ask, "How do we rob you?' To this God answers, "In tithes and offerings. You are under a curse." There is a curse for robbing God in tithes and offerings.

A year is twelve months, but there are some who:

- Give their tithes for no month and are thieves for twelve months.

- Give their tithes for one month and are thieves for eleven months.
- Give their tithes for two months and are thieves for ten months.
- Give their tithes for three months and are thieves for nine months.
- Give their tithes for four months and are thieves for eight months.
- Give their tithes for five months and are thieves for seven months.
- Give their tithes for six months and are thieves for six months.
- Give their tithes for seven months and are thieves for five months.
- Give their tithes for eight months and are thieves for four months.
- Give their tithes for nine months and are thieves for three months.
- Give their tithes for ten months and are thieves for two months.
- Give their tithes for eleven months and are thieves for one month.

What future can a thief from God have? What relationship with God can such a person have? If someone came into your house in January and stole. Then in February he came again to say he wants to stay with you, because he stole only once, will you take him in? May God tear the veil from the eyes of many; O God, tear the veil, tear the veil. Convict everyone reading these pages who has stolen for any number of months. Lord, convict your people, by the power of the Holy Spirit. Lord, convict them for their own good. o Lord, for their own good, so that the curse may be lifted. So that the curse on their spiritual life, on their financial life, on their academic life, on their social life and all the other domains may be lifted. Amen

8

THE CONSEQUENCES OF NOT TITHING

Some have cursed themselves with celibacy by robbing God. A girl may be very pretty, with very good character, but the curse will ensure that no one sees her. It may be a man. He too curses himself when he does not give his tithes. He may think that he is being smart, but he has cursed himself.

As you steal from God, thieves will come and steal from you. You will put the money into a bag with holes. There is celibacy as a curse and there is also joblessness as a curse. Take the case of someone who as a student, had an allowance from his parents. If during that time he stole God's tithes, he may realise that now he cannot find a job. He cursed himself and the extent of the curse is indescribable now.

The cursed person may have to buy drugs everyday as part of the curse. He may eat, but is always hungry, Food may lose its savour to a cursed person.

The cursed person reads the Bible, but all is cold. Revelations do not pop up. The cursed person finds that God is distant from him in the place of prayer. He may rattle a few sentences and then, doze off and wake up to rattle more sentences. There is no contact with God, no communion, no flow, because he stole God's tithe.

The children who used to do well in school may drop because their parents have stolen tithes. Nothing holds together for a man who has stolen tithes. He may look weary, cranky and old. It is as though old-age comes to him overnight. He may look as old as his grandfather. One woman said she was walking with her husband, then someone met them, greeted her husband and then asked, "Is this your mother?"[1] The woman who robs God may now look like the mother of her husband. It is a terrible thing to marry one's mother.

The one who steals from God finds that everything is punctured. He may build his house, enter before finishing, and in five years he is further away from finishing it than he was on the day he entered. Nothing has advanced. There may even be threats to take away the land from him.

When God goes to war against a man in his finances, it is total war. He just dislocates everything. All the doors are closed, and the man is under a curse.

9

BRING THE WHOLE TITHE

The Lord says, "Bring the whole tithe into the storehouse, that there may be food in my house." It is not only the tithe from your monthly salary, but the tithe that comes from every other source. Some make money from other sources, but only give the tithe of their salary. The tithe from mission allowances and from gifts received should be given as well. The whole tithe should be given into the storehouse. The local church constitutes the storehouse.

The tithes must be taken into the storehouse in time. You do not keep it to give two months at a time.

10

PUTTING GOD TO THE TEST–1

The Lord says that man should put Him to the test in this matter. He does not say man should put Him to the test through fiery prayers. He does not say that man should put Him to the test by fasting until he cannot walk without a stick. He does not say that man should put Him to the test by winning the whole city. If that were the case, you will say it is too difficult for you. It is simply, "Put me to the test in your tithes and offerings." He does not ask for something that is out of reach. He does not ask for something that is strange. He does not ask for what requires some extra quality for you to be able to obey.

What God is asking that I put Him to the test about is simple. Somebody gives me one hundred francs, ten francs is the tithe and five francs or another ten francs is the offering, and I am free, even though I had only one hundred francs. Take another example: somebody gives me one thousand francs: one hundred francs is the tithes, and any sum in addition to it is the offering, which I give to the Lord, and then I walk with a good conscience before God. Could anything be simpler?

11

FAITHFULNESS IN LITTLE THINGS

The truth is that the one who was not faithfully giving God ten francs out of every one hundred francs received, or one hundred francs out of every one thousand francs received, will find it difficult to give God one thousand francs when he receives ten thousand francs or ten thousand francs when he receives one hundred thousand francs. His whole world may collapse if he has to give God one hundred thousand francs when he receives one million.

If a man begins by being faithful in a little, it will be easier for him to continue. This is because a direction of flow has been established. Some people think that it will be easier for a millionaire to tithe. If you cannot give ten francs, how do you think that some other person will easily give one hundred thousand francs?

In one of the mission fields, there was a member of the assembly who was making many millions a month from working with an international organisation. He must have been earning about five million. When he gave his life to the

Lord Jesus, the missionary began to disciple him. They started with the tithe. The missionary told him he will have to give ten percent to the Lord. It was as if a whirl wind had fallen upon him. When the missionary insisted, he went and brought his budget for the five million, and asked from which budget line the five hundred thousand would come from.

He earned five million a month, but four million five hundred thousand seemed too small for him to live on. His wife was earning even more. The person who cannot be faithful in little things, can never handle larger issues.

12

THE BLESSING OF TITHING

The God of heaven says, "Test me in this." The God of heaven has commanded you and me to put Him to the test in our tithes and offerings. In giving Him the tithes and offerings, God promises the following in return: Test me in this and see if I will not throw open the floodgates of heaven and pour out so much blessing that you will not have room enough for it. I will prevent pests from devouring your crops, and the vines in your fields will not cast their fruit. "

There are floodgates in heaven. I say again that there are the floodgates of heaven. God says, "I will throw open the flood-gates of heaven and pour out so much blessing that you will not have room enough for it." God has promised. He further says, "Then all the nations will call you blessed, for yours will be a delightful land."

The passage continues as follows:

> *"You have said harsh things against me," says the Lord. "Yet you ask, 'What have we said against you?' "You have said, 'It is futile*

to serve God. What did we gain by carrying out his requirements and going about like mourners before the Lord Almighty? But now we call the arrogant blessed. Certainly the evil doers prosper, and even those who challenge God escape.'" Then those who feared God talked with each other, and the Lord listened and heard. A scroll of remembrance was written in his presence concerning those who feared the Lord and honoured his name. "They will be mine," says the Lord Almighty, "in the day when I make up my treasured possession. I will spare them, just as in compassion a man spares his son who serves him. And you will again see the distinction between the righteous and the wicked, between those who serve God and those who do not" (Malachi 3:13-18).

13

PUTTING GOD TO THE TEST—2

In my Bible I wrote down the many ways in which to put God to the test. On the 24th of October 1993, I wrote the following in my Bible: I put You, Lord, to the test, from this day, in the matter of giving You 83% of our income. Then the next year we moved to 84%. Then I went to a certain populous nation and I got the shock of my life. I was so shocked. I saw poverty in a way that paralysed me inside. I would see a man, his wife and their baby between them. Their home would be an umbrella. At another time, between the Airport and the main city, you saw people whose home was a tent made from spreading a raincoat. I was shocked to the depth of my being.

I was told what two hundred and fifty million people lived on. There are the top 25% that lived like the Americans. Then there is the middle class who live at different levels, and then a 25% that lived in abject poverty.

The top 25% are stinking rich. In one of the trips, I got to Bombay; the day after was a marriage. The man was one of those who are stinking-rich. He hired a jumbo jet and was flying for four hours over Bombay, while the marriage was taking place. The top four-hundred were having a feast as the plane was flying over the city. Then the next three days, he gave a feast for the ordinary people.

In India, a sister took me to their home. When we were talking, I said, "Your husband is a big businessman." She replied, "No! He is a merchant." She thought I had belittled the man in calling him a businessman. When their first daughter was twenty-one, she was made managing director of twelve companies. He had companies all over the world. The cream in India is really the cream. When I came back, I got those figures and we moved our giving to 90%. I told the Lord, "I put You to the test, o God, by giving You 90% of our income. You are the winner o God." This was in 1994. In 1996 we raised it to 91%. The year that followed, it became 91.5 %. Then my wife took her retirement benefits. It was eleven million four hundred thousand. I told the Lord, "My God, thank You for enabling us give You ten million six hundred and eighteen thousand francs as a single gift."

14

THE PROMISES OF GOD CANNOT BE BROKEN

What am I trying to say? I am trying to say that the promises of God cannot be broken. The Lord has asked that we test Him and see if He would not throw open the flood-gates of heaven. There are the floodgates of heaven.

Let me take the last two years. I told the Lord, "I put You to the test by giving You 100% of all ZTF and PZTF earned income from all sources and 90% of all ZTF and PZTF gifts from all people. So we gave God 100% of all our earned income and

90% of all cash gifts. Then I asked,

- God give Paul Tanee Fomum the gift of a wife,
- Stephen Tanee Fomum the gift of twelve new chemical compounds,
- Watchman Ndinteh the gift of twelve new chemical compounds,
- Money for Paul Fomum to finish the ground-floor of his house,

- Admission to second year for Mary Fomum, and Final year admission for John Fomum, and
- Reveal your choice of a wife for Stephen Tanee Fomum.

I have just read to you my dealings with God in this matter. This is because God says, "Test me in this." There are two more such dealings; the one of last year, and the one of this year.

I want to say that there is a living God. When God says, "Test me in this," He means it. When God says He will throw open the floodgates of heaven, He means it. There are actually the floodgates of heaven. I want to let you know that there are floodgates, floodgates, floodgates in heaven. If those floodgates do not exist, I challenge you, how is it that my wife and I gave God sixty-one million last year? If those floodgates do not exist - God has asked that we give Him seventy-five million this year - where will it come from? There is a living God. There is a living God. There is a living God, and He is the rewarder of those who diligently seek Him.

There is a living God.

There is a living God.

There is a living God, and He is the rewarder of those who diligently seek Him. He has promised: "Test me in this." He has asked that we test Him about that which is within reach, and see if He will not throw open the floodgates of heaven. God has asked me to give Him a single gift of fifty million this year. Last year we gave Him a single gift of twenty-five million.

15

IT IS NOT POSSIBLE FOR GOD TO LIE

I want to say, and I am saying it from lived experience, that it is not possible for God to lie. It is not possible for God to lie. It is not possible. It is not possible for God to lie. He says, "Test me in this"; about the tithe and the offering. See whether He will not throw open the floodgates of heaven, and pour out so much blessing, that you will not have room enough for it.

16

PUTTING GOD TO THE TEST–3

I have sometimes exposed the faults of my wife publicly. Let me say something to her favour. In 1967, we were students in Sierra Leone and engaged. Her pocket money was the equivalent of one pound sterling. There was the Sierra Leone Evangelical Fellowship meeting that brought together those who believed in the Lord. The convention went for three days. I remember it very clearly because of a message an American preached. He was preaching on the Lord telling His disciples to do what the Pharisees say, but not what they do (Matthew 23: 1-2).

When the offering came, my fiancée dropped the whole of her allowance for that month. I did not know it till three weeks later, when I found that she did not have her basic supplies. She was one-year-old in the Lord when she put in all her pocket money. It is part of the reason why we are where we are now in giving to God. I do not know what she saw of God then to let all of a month's allowance go. Again it says, when you are not faithful in small matters, you will fail when big issues come. But if you will be faithful in small matters, you will build the character that will stand the test of major issues.

17

THE SCRIPTURE CANNOT BE BROKEN

In John 10:35 we read :

> *"If he called them 'gods,' to whom the word of God came - and the Scripture cannot be broken."*

The Scripture cannot be broken.

Say it with me: The Scripture cannot be broken. Which Scripture was the Lord Jesus talking about? He was talking about the Old Testament Scripture. Jesus in His life-time saw no New Testament Scripture. The Scripture about which the Lord Jesus Christ is talking is the Old Testament Scripture.

There are some counterfeit people now in town who say tithing is of the Old Testament and not applicable to the New Testament believer. The Bible says: He said to them,

> *"This is what I told you while I was still with you: Everything must be fulfilled that is written about me in the Law of Moses, the Prophets and the Psalms"* (Luke 24: 44.)

The Lord Jesus was talking about the Old Testament Scripture!!!

18

JESUS AND THE TEACHING ON TITHES

Some people say that Jesus said nothing about tithing. Look at what follows:

> *Woe to you, teachers of the Law and Pharisees, you hypocrites! You give a tenth of your spices - mint, dill and cumin. But you have neglected the more important matters of the Law - justice, mercy and faithfulness. You should have practised the latter, without neglecting the former (Matthew 23:23).*

He was saying, you are to practice justice, mercy and faithfulness without neglecting tithing the mint, dill and cumin. These are the words of the Supreme Lord.

It was nowhere in the Lord's thinking, that anyone could go without giving tithes and offerings; if that happens, He would be contradicting the Scripture which He quotes. The Lord Jesus Christ is the Author of the Scripture, from Genesis to Revelation. The Lord taught that the tithe was to be given.

19

THE GENESIS OF TITHING

The tithe, in human experience, is recorded for the first time in Genesis 14: 18-20:

> *Then Melchizedek king of Salem brought out bread and wine. He was priest of God Most High, and he blessed Abram, saying, "Blessed be Abram by God Most High, Creator of heaven and earth. And blessed be God Most High, who delivered your enemies into your hand." Then Abram gave him a tenth of everything.*

Abraham gave the tithe. It was just near the beginning of his walk with God. He gave Him a tenth of everything. It was not a tenth of some things. It was a tenth of everything.

20

THE LAW OF TITHES AND OFFERINGS

What Abraham did was not the law. It was life. The law came in Exodus chapter 20, after Abraham, Isaac, Jacob, then the departure to Egypt, the 430 years of stay in Egypt, and then on coming back at Sinai, there was the law. Tithes and offerings are rooted in the relationship with God. It was the overflow of gratitude.

21

TITHING AS GRATITUDE TO GOD

When God blesses a man with salvation, the man responds with a tithe and an offering. We may represent it as below;

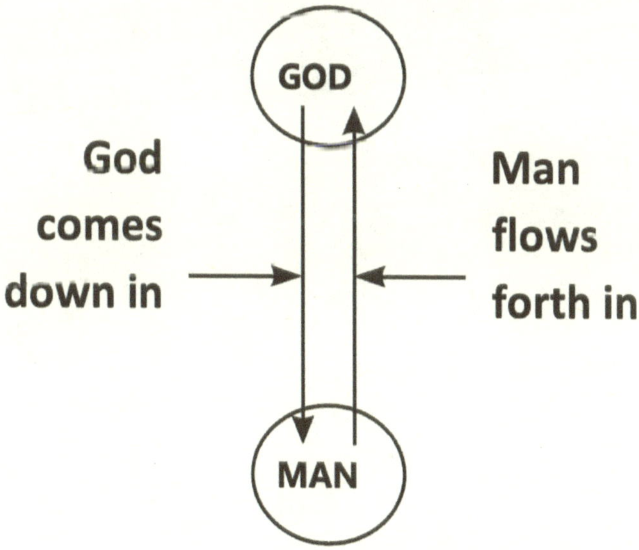

God comes down in salvation to pick up a hopeless, helpless man, fit for hell, as you and I are by nature. He picks us up and makes us His. Then our response is the tithe and the offering. How can that be removed, unless you want to remove the salvation as well? Tithing and offering is the overflow of gratitude for God-given salvation.

22

THE BARGAINER'S CASE

When the bargaining Jacob found God at Bethel, we read,

> *Then Jacob made a vow saying, 'If God will be with me and will watch over me on this journey I am taking and will give me food to eat and clothes to wear so that I return safely to my father's house, then the Lord will be my God and this stone that I have set up as a pillar will be God's house, and of all that you give me, I will give you a tenth* (Genesis 28:20-22).

Jacob was saying, "Where there is God's house, a tithe should be given." He was acknowledging what his father had already lived - that where there is the house of God, the tithe should be given.

23

TITHING AND THE LOCAL CHURCH

We have said from the example of Abraham and Jacob that where there is the house of God, the tithe should be given. The tithe belongs to the local church. You can give the offering to the ministry, but the tithe must be given to the local church, as gratitude to the Lord.

24

BE YOUR BROTHER'S KEEPER

If you love somebody, then at all cost you should get him to give his tithes, in order to flee from a curse. At all cost, get the person to tithe, for the person's good, so that he may not be under a curse (Malachi 3: 8-9). It is saving the person from a curse. Can you love somebody and allow him to settle under a curse? If you love someone, then at all cost, you should get him to give the tithe and so have the floodgates of heaven open to him (Malachi 3: 10).

25

PARENTS, CHILDREN AND TITHING

How can a father and a mother be at peace with children who are not tithing, knowing that these children will do themselves untold harm? Should they not take all measures, because of a vision of what the children must become, to ensure that from the day they are converted, there is no month they do not give a tithe? It is compelling to the parents, to do everything possible so that their children cause God to open the floodgates of heaven, and pour overflowing blessings that they cannot all contain.

26

THE SHEPHERD, HIS FLOCK AND TITHING

How can a shepherd, who loves his flock ensure that each sheep in the flock he shepherds escapes the curse? Do you not force things on your children, which they do not want to do? Because you know better, you force them for their own good. The shepherd should do the same for the flock under his care.

Why do the leaders not say, "Marry anybody, we will close our eyes and just bless?" Why do they say, "No", to some who want to get married to the wrong persons? It is because of love. They know what will happen after that. Out of love they say, "No!" So then, compelling everybody to give the tithe, so that they may flee the curse, is a manifestation of the shepherd's love for the flock.

How can a pastor settle to have a part of his flock under a curse? How can a disciple-maker settle and be happy when some of his disciples are under a curse? It is compelling to the pastors and to the disciple-makers, to do everything possible so that their people cause God to open the floodgates of heaven, and pour overflowing blessings that they cannot all contain. In this manner, the church will come back to God. They will return to loving God. They will return to:

- Prayer,
- Bible reading,
- Evangelism,
- Seeking God,
- Finding God,
- Knowing God,
- Loving God,
- Flowing out to God and
- Brotherly fellowship.

When this is done, all the other blessings will come upon the church, and flow from the church to the nations.

27

THE DEBTOR AND TITHING

If you are in debt, do not make your case worse by holding back the tithe. You will rather sink deeper. Tithing will place you under God's favour and blessing.

Tuesday, 7th February 2006
Obili.

BACK MATTERS

VERY IMPORTANT!!!

If you have not yet received Jesus as your Lord and Saviour, I encourage you to receive Him. Here are some steps to help you,

ADMIT that you are a sinner by nature and by practice and that on your own you are without hope. Tell God you have personally sinned against Him in your thoughts, words and deeds. Confess your sins to Him, one after another in a sincere prayer. Do not leave out any sins that you can remember. Truly turn from your sinful ways and abandon them. If you stole, steal no more. If you have been committing adultery or fornication, stop it. God will not forgive you if you have no desire to stop sinning in all areas of your life, but if you are sincere, He will give you the power to stop sinning.

BELIEVE that Jesus Christ, who is God's Son, is the only Way, the only Truth and the only Life. Jesus said,

> *"I am the way, the truth and the life; no one comes to the Father, but by me" (John 14:6).*

The Bible says,

> *"For there is one God, and there is one mediator between God and men, the man Christ Jesus, who gave himself as a ransom for all" (1 Timothy 2:5-6).*

> *"And there is salvation in no one else (apart from Jesus), for there is no other name under heaven given among men by which we must be saved" (Acts 4:12).*

> *But to all who received him, who believed in his name, he gave power to become children of God..." (John 1:12).*

BUT,

CONSIDER the cost of following Him. Jesus said that all who follow Him must deny themselves, and this includes selfish financial, social and other interests. He also wants His followers to take up their crosses and follow Him. Are you prepared to abandon your own interests daily for those of Christ? Are you prepared to be led in a new direction by Him? Are you prepared to suffer for Him and die for Him if need be? Jesus will have nothing to do with half-hearted people. His demands are total. He will only receive and forgive those who are prepared to follow Him AT ANY COST. Think about it and count the cost. If you are prepared to follow Him, come what may, then there is something to do.

INVITE Jesus to come into your heart and life. He says,

> *"Behold I stand at the door and knock. If anyone hears my voice and opens the door (to his heart and life), I will come in to him and eat with him, and he with me"* (Revelation 3:20).

Why don't you pray a prayer like the following one or one of your own construction as the Holy Spirit leads?

> "Lord Jesus, I am a wretched, lost sinner who has sinned in thought, word and deed. Forgive all my sins and cleanse me. Receive me, Saviour and transform me into a child of God. Come into my heart now and give me eternal life right now. I will follow you at all costs, trusting the Holy Spirit to give me all the power I need."

When you pray this prayer sincerely, Jesus answers at once and justifies you before God and makes you His child.

> *Please write to us (**ztfbooks@cmfionline.org**) and I will pray for you and help you as you go on with Jesus Christ.*

THANK YOU

For Reading This Book

If you have any question and/or need help, do not hesitate to contact us through ztfbooks@cmfionline.org. If the book has blessed you, then we would also be grateful if you leave a positive review at your favorite retailer.

ZTF BOOKS, through Christian Publishing House (CPH) offers a wide selection of best selling Christian books (in print, eBook & audiobook formats) on a broad spectrum of topics, including marriage & family, sexuality, practical spiritual warfare, Christian service, Christian leadership, and much more. Visit us at ztfbooks.com to learn more about our latest releases and special offers. And thank you for being a ZTF BOOK reader.

We invite you to connect with more from the author through social media (cmfionline) and/or ministry website (ztfministry.org), where we offer both on-ground and remote training courses (all year round) from basic to university level at the University of Prayer and Fasting (WUPF) and the School of Knowing and Serving God (SKSG). You are highly welcome to enrol at your soonest convenience. A FREE online Bible Course is also available.

We would like to recommend to you another book on the same theme - *Giving to God*:

Do you find yourself questioning why God's children often struggle in poverty, while worldly wealth thrives around them?

In *Giving to God*, Z.T. Fomum unveils a revolutionary perspective on prosperity and faith. This transformative sermon offers a roadmap to align your financial journey with God's principles, unlocking spiritual growth and abundant blessings along the way.

Drawing from the treasures of Scripture and the wisdom of generations, Fomum dismantles common misconceptions about money and spirituality. Through biblical insights and practical wisdom, he illuminates how embracing God's ways of handling finances leads to spiritual enrichment, healthier relationships, and eternal rewards.

Inside, you'll discover:

- The truth behind money's role in your spiritual journey.
- How giving to God aligns your heart with divine purpose.
- Practical strategies for managing your finances as a faithful steward.
- The eternal impact of financial decisions on your relationship with God.

- Lessons from Biblical figures and contemporary spiritual leaders who embraced God's financial principles.

Giving to God is more than a book—it's a transformative manual to realigning your financial life with God's intentions. Whether you're seeking spiritual growth, godly financial management principles, or a deeper connection with God, this book offers the guidance you need to navigate the realm of finances with grace and purpose.

ABOUT THE AUTHOR

Professor Zacharias Tanee Fomum was born in the flesh on 20th June 1945 and became born again on 13th June 1956. On 1st October 1966, He consecrated his life to the Lord Jesus and to His service, and was filled with the Holy Spirit on 24th October 1970. He was taken to be with the Lord on 14th March, 2009.

Pr Fomum was admitted to a first class in the Bachelor of Science degree, graduating as a prize winning student from Fourah Bay College in the University of Sierra Leone in October 1969. At the age of 28, he was awarded a Ph.D. in Organic Chemistry by the University of Makerere, Kampala in Uganda. In October 2005, he was awarded a Doctor of Science (D.Sc) by the University of Durham, Great Britain. This higher doctorate was in recognition of his distinct contributions to scientific knowledge through research. As a Professor of Organic Chemistry in the University of Yaoundé 1, Cameroon, Professor Fomum supervised or co-supervised more than 100 Master's Degree and Doctoral Degree theses and co-authored over 160 scientific articles in leading international journals. He considered Jesus Christ the Lord of Science ("For by Him all things were created..." – Colossians 1:16), and scientific research an act of obedience to God's command to "subdue the earth" (Genesis 1:28). He therefore made the Lord Jesus the Director of his research laboratory while he took the place of deputy director, and attributed his outstanding success as a scientist to Jesus' revelational leadership.

In more than 40 years of Christian ministry, Pr Fomum travelled extensively, preaching the Gospel, planting churches and training spiritual leaders. He made more than:

- 700 missionary journeys within Cameroon, which ranged from one day to three weeks in duration.
- 500 missionary journeys to more than 70 different nations in all the six continents. These ranged from two days to six weeks in duration.

By the time of his going to be with the Lord in 2009, he had preached in over 1000 localities in Cameroon, sent over 200 national missionaries into many localities in Cameroon and planted over 1300 churches in the various administrative provinces of Cameroon. At his base in Yaoundé, he planted and built a mega-church with his co-workers which grew to a steady membership of about 12,000. Pr Fomum was the founding team-leader of Christian Missionary Fellowship International (CMFI); an evangelism, soul-winning, disciple making, Church-planting and missionary-sending movement with more than 200 international missionaries and thousands of churches in 65 nations spread across Africa, Europe, the Americas, Asia and Oceania. In the course of their ministry, Pr Fomum and his team witnessed more than 10,000 recorded healing miracles performed by God in answer to prayer in the name of Jesus Christ. These miracles include instant healings of headaches, cancers, HIV/AIDS, blindness, deafness, dumbness, paralysis, madness, and new teeth and organs received.

Pr Fomum read the entire Bible more than 60 times, read more than 1350 books on the Christian faith and authored over 150 books to advance the Gospel of Jesus Christ. 5 million copies of these books are in circulation in 12 languages as well as 16 million gospel tracts in 17 languages.

Pr Fomum was a man who sought God. He spent between 15 minutes and six hours daily alone with God in what he called Daily Dynamic Encounters with God (DDEWG). During these DDEWG he read God's Word, meditated on it, listened to God's voice, heard God speak to him, recorded what God was saying to him and prayed it through. He thus had over 18,000 DDEWG. He also had over 60 periods of withdrawing to seek God alone for periods that ranged from 3 to 21 days (which he termed Retreats for Spiritual Progress). The time he spent seeking God slowly transformed him into a man who hungered, thirsted and panted after God. His unceasing heart cry was: "Oh, that I would have more of God!"

Pr Fomum was a man of prayer and a leading teacher on prayer in many churches and conferences around the world. He considered prayer to be the most important work that can be done for God and for man. He was a man of faith who believed that God answers prayer. He kept a record of his prayer requests and had over 50, 000 recorded answers to prayer in his prayer books. He carried out over 100 Prayer Walks of between five and forty-seven kilometres in towns and cities around the world. He and his team carried out over 57 Prayer Crusades (periods of forty days and nights during which at least eight hours are invested into prayer each day). They also carried out over 80 Prayer Sieges (times of near non-stop praying that ranges from 24 hours to 120 hours). He authored the Prayer Power Series, a 13-volume set of books on various aspects of prayer; Supplication, Fasting, Intercession and Spiritual Warfare. He started prayer chains, prayer rooms, prayer houses, national and continental prayer movements in Cameroon and other nations. He worked with leaders of local churches in India to disciple and train more than 2 million believers.

Pr Fomum also considered fasting as one of the weapons of Christian Spiritual Warfare. He carried out over 250 fasts ranging from three days to forty days, drinking only water or water supplemented with soluble vitamins. Called by the Lord to a distinct ministry of intercession, he pioneered fasting and prayer movements and led in battles against principalities and powers obstructing the progress of the Gospel and God's global purposes. He was enabled to carry out 3 supra – long fasts of between 52 and 70 days in his final years.

Pr Fomum chose a lifestyle of simplicity and "self- imposed poverty" in order to invest more funds into the critical work of evangelism, soul winning, church-planting and the building up of believers. Knowing the importance of money and its role in the battle to reach those without Christ with the glorious Gospel, he and his wife grew to investing 92.5% of their earned income from all sources (salaries, allowances, royalties and cash gifts) into the Gospel. They invested with the hope that, as they grew in the knowledge and the love of the Lord, and the perishing souls of people, they would one day invest 99% of their income into the Gospel.

He was married to Prisca Zei Fomum and they had seven children who are all involved in the work of the Gospel, some serving as missionaries. Prisca is a national and international minister, specializing in the winning and discipling of children to Jesus Christ. She also communicates and imparts the vision of ministry to children with a view to raising and building up ministers to them.

The Professor owed all that he was and all that God had done through him, to the unmerited favour and blessing of God and to his worldwide army of friends and co-workers. He considered himself nothing without them and the blessing of God; and would have amounted to nothing but for them. All praise and glory to Jesus Christ!

facebook.com/cmfionline
twitter.com/cmfionline
instagram.com/cmfionline
pinterest.com/cmfionline
youtube.com/cmfionline

RECOMMENDED BOOKS

https://ztfbooks.com

THE CHRISTIAN WAY

1. The Way Of Life
2. The Way Of Obedience
3. The Way Of Discipleship
4. The Way Of Sanctification
5. The Way Of Christian Character
6. The Way Of Spiritual Power
7. The Way Of Christian Service
8. The Way Of Spiritual Warfare
9. The Way Of Suffering For Christ
10. The Way Of Victorious Praying
11. The Way Of Overcomers
12. The Way Of Spiritual Encouragement
13. The Way Of Loving The Lord

THE PRAYER POWER SERIES

1. The Way Of Victorious Praying
2. The Ministry Of Fasting
3. The Art Of Intercession
4. The Practice Of Intercession
5. Praying With Power
6. Practical Spiritual Warfare Through Prayer
7. Moving God Through Prayer
8. The Ministry Of Praise And Thanksgiving

9. Waiting On The Lord In Prayer
10. The Ministry Of Supplication
11. Life-Changing Thoughts On Prayer (Vol. 1)
12. The Centrality of Prayer
13. Life-Changing Thoughts On Prayer (Vol. 2)
14. Prayer and Spiritual Intimacy
15. Life-Changing Thoughts on Prayer (Vol. 3)
16. The Art of Worship
17. Life-Changing Thoughts on Prayer (Vol. 4)
18. Life-Changing Thoughts on Prayer (Vol. 5)
19. Learning to Importune in Prayer
20. Prayer And A Walk With God
21. From His Prayer files
22. Prayer and Holiness
23. Practical Helps in Fasting Long Fasts
24. Life-Changing Thoughts on Fasting (Vol 1)
25. Life-Changing Thoughts on Fasting (Vol 2)
26. Pray Without Ceasing
27. Pray or Perish

PRACTICAL HELPS FOR OVERCOMERS

1. Discipleship at any cost
2. The Use Of Time
3. Retreats For Spiritual Progress
4. Personal Spiritual Revival
5. Daily Dynamic Encounters With God
6. The School Of Truth
7. How To Succeed In The Christian Life
8. The Christian And Money
9. Deliverance From The Sin Of Laziness
10. The Art Of Working Hard

11. Knowing God - The Greatest Need Of The Hour
12. Restitution - An Important Message For The Overcomers
13. Revelation: A Must
14. The Overcomer As A Servant Of Man
15. True Repentance
16. You Can Receive A Pure Heart Today
17. You Can Lead Someone To The Lord Jesus Today
18. You Can Receive The Baptism Into The Holy Spirit Now
19. The Dignity Of Manual Labour
20. You Have A Talent!
21. The Making Of Disciples
22. The Secret Of Spiritual Fruitfulness
23. Are You Still A Disciple Of The Lord Jesus?
24. Who Is Truly a Disciple of The Lord Jesus?

LEADING GOD'S PEOPLE

1. Vision, Burden, Action
2. Knowing The God Of Unparalleled Goodness
3. Brokenness: The Secret Of Spiritual Overflow
4. The Secret Of Spiritual Rest
5. Spiritual Aggressiveness
6. The Character And The Personality of The Leader
7. Leading A Local Church
8. The Leader And His God
9. Revolutionary Thoughts On Spiritual Leadership
10. Leading God's People
11. Laws Of Spiritual Leadership
12. Laws Of Spiritual Success, Volume 1
13. The Shepherd And The Flock

14. Basic Christian Leadership
15. A Missionary life and a missionary heart
16. Spiritual Nobility
17. Spiritual Leadership in the Pattern of David
18. The Heart Surgery for the Potential Minister of the Gospel
19. Prerequisites For Spiritual Ministry
20. Power For Service
21. In The Crucible For Service
22. Qualifications For Serving in The Gospel
23. You, Your Team, And Your Ministry
24. Church Planting Strategies
25. Critical Ingredients for Successful Spiritual Leadership
26. The Power of a Man's All

GOD, SEX AND YOU

1. Enjoying The Premarital Life
2. Enjoying The Choice Of Your Marriage Partner
3. Enjoying The Married Life
4. Divorce And Remarriage
5. A Successful Marriage; The Husband's Making
6. A Successful Marriage; The Wife's Making
7. Life-changing Thoughts On Marriage

OFF-SERIES

1. Inner Healing
2. No Failure Needs To Be Final
3. Facing Life's Problems Victoriously
4. A Word To The Students

5. Blessings and Curses
6. Spiritual Fragrance (Volume 1)
7. Roots And Destinies
8. Walking With God (Vol. 1)
9. God Centredness
10. Victorious Dispositions
11. The Processes Of Faith
12. The Spirit-Filled Life
13. God, Money, And You
14. Knowing God And Walking With Him
15. Knowing and Serving God (Volume 2)
16. Esther
17. The Church: Rights And Responsibilities of The Believer
18. Children in God's Eternal Purposes
19. Giving to God
20. Relationship and Intimacy With God
21. Treasures in Heaven

PRACTICAL HELPS IN SANCTIFICATION

1. Deliverance From Sin
2. The Way Of Sanctification
3. Sanctified And Consecrated For Spiritual Ministry
4. The Sower, The Seed, And The Hearts Of Men
5. Freedom From The Sin Of Adultery And Fornication
6. The Sin Before You May Lead To Immediate Death: Do Not Commit It!
7. Be Filled With The Holy Spirit
8. The Power Of The Holy Spirit In The Winning Of The Lost

9. Deliverance from the Sin of Gluttony
10. A Vessel of Honour
11. The Believer's Conscience
12. Practical Dying to Self and the Spirit-filled Life
13. Issues of The Heart
14. Rebellion

MAKING SPIRITUAL PROGRESS

1. The Ministers And The Ministry of The New Covenant
2. The Cross In The Life And Ministry Of The Believer
3. Making Spiritual Progress, Volume 1
4. Making Spiritual Progress, Volume 2
5. Making Spiritual Progress, Volume 3
6. Making Spiritual Progress, Volume 4
7. Moving on With The Lord Jesus Christ
8. The Narrow Way (Volume 1)
9. Making Spiritual Progress (Volumes 1-4)

EVANGELISM

1. 36 Reasons For Winning The Lost To Christ
2. Soul Winning, Volume 1
3. Soul Winning, Volume 2
4. The Winning of The Lost as Life's Supreme Task
5. Salvation And Soul-Winning
6. Soul Winning And The Making Of Disciples
7. Victorious Soul-Winning

GOD LOVES YOU

1. God's Love And Forgiveness
2. The Way Of Life
3. Come Back Home My Son; I Still Love You
4. Jesus Loves You And Wants To Heal You
5. Come And See; Jesus Has Not Changed!
6. Celebrity A Mask
7. Encounter The Saviour
8. Meet The Liberator
9. Jesus Saves And Heals Today
10. Jesus is The Answer

WOMEN OF THE GLORY

1. The Secluded Worshipper: Prophetess Anna
2. Unending Intimacy: Mary of Bethany
3. Winning Love: Mary Magdalene

ZTF COMPLETE WORKS

1. The School of Soul Winners and Soul Winning
2. The Complete Works of Z.T.F on Holiness (Volume 1)
3. The Complete Works of Z.T.F on Basic Christian Doctrine
4. The Complete Works of Z.T.F on Marriage (Volume 1)
5. The Complete Works of Z.T.F on The Gospel Message (Volume 1)
6. The Complete Works of Z.T.F on Prayer (Volume 1)

7. The Complete Works of Z.T.F on Prayer (Volume 2)
8. The Complete Works of Z.T.F on Prayer (Volume 3)
9. The Complete Works of Z.T.F on Prayer (Volume 4)
10. The Complete Works of Z.T.F on Prayer (Volume 5)
11. The Complete Works of Z.T.F on Leadership (Volume 1)
12. The Complete Works of Z.T.F on Leadership (Volume 2)
13. The Complete Works of Z.T.F on Leadership (Volume 3)

SPECIAL SERIES

1. A Broken Vessel
2. The Joy of Begging to Belong to the Lord Jesus Christ: A Testimony
3. Separation from the common

ZTF AUTO-BIOGRAPHIES

1. From His Lips: About The Author
2. From His Lips: About His Co-Workers
3. From His Lips: Back From His Missions
4. From His Lips: About Our Ministry
5. From His Lips: On Our Vision
6. From His Lips: The work is the worker
7. From His Lips: The Battles He Fought
8. From His Lips: The Authority And Power of His Life
9. From His Lips: The Influences That Moulded Him: People And Books

THE OVERTHROW OF PRINCIPALITIES

1. Deliverance From Demons
2. The Prophecy Of The Overthrow Of The Satanic Prince Of Cameroon
3. The Prophecy of the Overthrow of The Satanic Prince of Yaounde
4. The Prophecy of the Overthrow of The Satanic Prince of Douala
5. The overthrow of principalities and powers
6. From His Lips: The Battles He Fought

CONTINUOUS PERSONAL SPIRITUAL REVIVAL

1. Victorious Proclamations

OTHER BOOKS

1. The Missionary as a Son
2. What Our Ministry is
3. Conserver la Moisson
4. Disciples of Jesus Christ to Make Disciples For Jesus Christ
5. The House Church in God's Eternal Purposes
6. Christian Maturation
7. Heroes of the Kingdom
8. Spiritual Leadership in the Pattern of Gideon
9. The School of Evangelism
10. A Good Minister of Jesus Christ
11. Building a Spiritual Nation: The Foundation
12. Building a Spiritual Nation: Spiritual Statesmanship

13. Removing Obstacles Through Prayer and Fasting
14. The Chronicles of Our Ministry
15. The Making of Disciples: The Master's Way
16. Watching in Prayer
17. The Character of the Christian Worker
18. Church and Mission
19. Strategic Missionary Work

DISTRIBUTORS OF ZTF BOOKS

These books can be obtained in French and English Language from any of the following distribution outlets:

EDITIONS DU LIVRE CHRETIEN (ELC)

- **Location:** Paris, France
- **Email:** editionlivrechretien@gmail.com
- **Phone:** +33 6 98 00 90 47

INTERNET

- **Location:** on all major online **eBook, Audiobook** and **print-on-demand** (paperback) retailers.
- **Email**: ztfbooks@cmfionline.org
- **Phone**: +47 454 12 804
- **Website**: ztfbooks.com

CPH YAOUNDE

- **Location:** Yaounde, Cameroon
- **Email:** editionsztf@gmail.com
- **Phone:** +237 74756559

ZTF LITERATURE AND MEDIA HOUSE

- **Location:** Lagos, Nigeria
- **Email:** zlmh@ztfministry.org
- **Phone:** +2348152163063

CPH BURUNDI

- **Location:** Bujumbura, Burundi
- **Email:** cph-burundi@ztfministry.org
- **Phone:** +257 79 97 72 75

CPH UGANDA

- **Location:** Kampala, Uganda
- **Email:** cph-uganda@ztfministry.org
- **Phone:** +256 785 619613

CPH SOUTH AFRICA

- **Location:** Johannesburg, RSA
- **Email:** tantohtantoh@yahoo.com
- **Phone**: +27 83 744 5682

NOTES

6. TITHING

1. This percentage includes those who gave, whether it was the full tithe or not, for one month or more. If we take the case of those who gave the full tithe, every month, the percentage will be much lower. It could be 22.5%

8. THE CONSEQUENCES OF NOT TITHING

1. This story is found in the book *Billy Graham Answers your Questions*

www.ingramcontent.com/pod-product-compliance
Lightning Source LLC
LaVergne TN
LVHW090428210926
848480LV00002B/737